Spike
the Concert

June Crebbin

Illustrated by Peter Kavanagh

CAMBRIDGE
UNIVERSITY PRESS

Jess picked up her violin and began to play. She liked
to practise in the morning, before she went to school.

From her bedroom window, she could see the way
that Emma would come from next door to call for her.
They always went to school together.

She played 'Jingle Bells' twice, and then started 'Silent Night'. That was more difficult. But she had been practising it every day for two weeks now. She wanted it to be just right for the concert that afternoon. Dad said that it was an honour to be chosen to play on her own.

She glanced out of the window to see if Emma was coming, and was horrified to see Spike going out onto the road.

Jess flew downstairs. "Spike's out again," she shouted. "He's out on the road."

She tore out through the front door, with Dad and Alice close behind her.

Spike was on the other side of the road.

"Don't call him," said Dad, "or he'll run across the road."
He waited until there was a break in the traffic. "You stay
here," he said. "I'll get him."

Jess and Alice waited.

Emma came out of her front gate, carrying a recorder.
"What's the matter?" she said.

"Spike's out on the road," said Jess. "He must have
squeezed through the hole in the side fence."

"One minute he was in the back garden," said Alice,
"and the next, he wasn't."

Dad came back, holding Spike by the collar. "I *will* mend that fence," he said. "I promise."

"Today?" said Jess.

"Yes," said Dad.

They all went indoors. Jess looked at the clock. "There's still time to practise before we go," she said.

"Good," said Emma. "I came early so I could hear your pieces."

Spike bounded up the stairs with them. But Jess stopped him.

"Call him, Alice," she said. "You know what he's like when I'm practising."

Emma giggled. "That would never do," she said.

Alice called him, and Spike slid reluctantly down the stairs.

Jess played both her pieces of music right through. Emma sat on the bed. "You're really good," she said. "I wish I could play like that."

"You're really good on your recorder," said Jess. She was in the recorder group too. But she had been playing the violin since she was four. She'd started on a special small one that had been Dad's when he was young. Now she had her own.

"I can't wait until this afternoon," said Emma, as they
set off for school.

"Neither can I," said Jess.

The concert was to be held on the other side of town,
in a church hall. It was a Christmas concert especially for
the old people. The children were going to walk there and
back, so they would be out for the whole afternoon.

"Are you nervous?" said Emma. "I'd be nervous if I had to play on my own."

"A bit," said Jess, "but I'm all right once I get started." She had practised her pieces at school with her teacher. Mrs Fraser played the piano part while Jess played the violin part.

Mrs Fraser was very kind. She always nodded her head at exactly the right moment for Jess to start playing. And if Jess went a little bit slower in places, Mrs Fraser went a little bit slower too.

After lunch, everyone who was going to be in the concert set off. Some mums and dads went with them.

Soon they reached the centre of town. It was very busy. They had to cross the main road in groups at the traffic lights.

As they were passing the Town Hall, Emma said, "That looks just like Spike over there."

Jess looked. "It *is* Spike," she said. As she watched, Spike stepped off the pavement onto the road and a car had to brake hard to miss him.

"SPIKE, STAY!" shouted Jess. But the traffic was too noisy for Spike to hear her. He came right across the road.

By now, all the children behind Jess had stopped. Spike didn't see Jess at first. He was too busy wagging his tail and leaping up and down at the back of the line.

"SPIKE, COME HERE!" shouted Jess. Spike heard her and came to her. But he didn't wag his tail. He slunk towards her with his tail between his legs. He knew that he shouldn't be out by himself.

Everyone near Jess crowded round, wanting to see Spike and stroke him. The children in front of her had stopped too. Mrs Fraser came from the front of the line to see what was happening.

"It's my dog," explained Jess. She felt a bit better now that Spike was standing safely beside her. But her voice wobbled. She had been so frightened, seeing him cross the road in between all those cars.

"What's he doing here?" said Mrs Fraser.

Jess explained about the hole in the fence. She kept a firm hold of Spike's collar while she talked.

Mrs Fraser looked at her watch. "Well, he'll have to come with us," she decided. "We can't leave him here."

"I'll look after him," said Jess quickly. "There's just one thing . . ."

But Mrs Fraser had already moved forward to take her place at the front of the line and she didn't hear Jess.

Once again, the line of children moved forward.

"But what about Spike at the concert?" said Emma.

"I don't know," said Jess. She would have to speak to Mrs Fraser about Spike before she played her violin.

The hall was beginning to fill up as they arrived. Everyone was delighted to see the children and Spike.

Spike was all right at the moment. He was lying down underneath one of the mums' chairs on the front row. But Jess was getting worried.

Mrs Fraser was putting up music stands, arranging her
music on the piano and showing the choir where to sit.
It was impossible to get near her.

Jess took her place in the choir.

"Now," smiled Mrs Fraser. "Is everyone ready?" Jess put up her hand. But Mrs Fraser had turned away to speak to the lady in charge. "We're all ready," said Mrs Fraser, and she went over to the piano.

First the choir sang some carols. Then a boy played the flute. Then the recorder group played some carols and then two girls played a duet on their clarinets.

Everything went well. After each piece, the audience clapped loudly.

Then it was time for Jess to play her violin. She put her
music on the stand. Perhaps she could speak to Mrs Fraser now.

But the whole room was quiet, watching. Everyone was
watching and waiting. At the piano, Mrs Fraser was waiting.
Jess tucked her violin under her chin. There was nothing else
she could do. She would have to play.

Out of the corner of her eye, she saw Spike quietly stand and make his way towards her. Mrs Fraser couldn't see him. At the piano, she smiled and nodded. It was the signal for Jess to begin.

By now Spike had reached her. He sat down.

Jess started to play.

By her side, Spike put his head back and howled. Mrs Fraser almost stopped playing.

But not Jess. Once she had started, she kept going. And Spike kept howling.

The hall became very still.

At the end of the piece, there was a moment's pause.
Then there was a storm of clapping, and someone shouted,
"Bravo! Bravo!"

Mrs Fraser hurried across to Jess. "Are you all right?"
she whispered.

"Yes," said Jess. "I did try and tell you. Spike always howls
when I play my violin. I'm used to it." But she wasn't used to
it in front of a roomful of people. Her hands were shaking.

"You did very well," said Mrs Fraser.

The mum who had been looking after Spike came forward.

"Sorry," she said. "Shall I take him out?"

"Yes please," said Mrs Fraser. "Now, are you all right for your second piece?" she said to Jess.

"I think so," said Jess.

She played it beautifully, and everyone clapped loudly when she had finished.

That evening, when Dad came to fetch Jess and Alice from Emma's house, he was very pleased to see Spike there too. He'd worried about him all day.

"I was mending the fence," he explained, "and the milkman came, so I went to pay him. When I came back, Spike had gone."

Jess told him her story as they went home. "And you know what he's like," she said. "He howled all the time I was playing."

"Oh dear," said Dad.

"But only during my first piece," said Jess. "A lady took
him out before I played my second piece."

"Just as well," said Dad. He grinned. "It wouldn't have been
a very 'Silent Night' with Spike there, would it?"